[handwritten signature] April 2013

LESS OF HER

The publication of this book is supported by a grant
from the Greenwall Fund of The Academy of American Poets

The New Issues Press Poetry Series

Editor	Herbert Scott
Associate Editor	David Dodd Lee
Advisory Editors	Nancy Eimers, Mark Halliday William Olsen, J. Allyn Rosser
Assistant to the Editor	Rebecca Beech
Assistant Editors	Allegra Blake, Matthew Hollrah, Alexander Long, Amy McInnis, Tony Spicer, Tom West
Editorial Assistants	Laura Maloney, Lydia Melvin, Bonnie Wozniak
Business Manager	Michele McLaughlin
Fiscal Officer	Marilyn Rowe

The New Issues Press Poetry Series is sponsored by The College
of Arts and Sciences, Western Michigan University, Kalamazoo, Michigan

An Inland Seas Poetry Book

 Inland Seas poetry books are supported by a grant from
The Michigan Council for Arts and Cultural Affairs.

First Edition, 1999.

ISBN: 0-9382826-81-4 (casebound)
0-9382826-82-2 (paperbound)

Library of Congress Cataloging-in-Publication Data:
McLain, Paula
Less of Her / Paula McLain
Library of Congress Catalog Card Number (99-070683)

Art Direction:	Tricia Hennessy
Design:	Andrea Sepic
Production:	Paul Sizer The Design Center, Department of Art College of Fine Arts Western Michigan University
Printing:	Courier Corporation

LESS OF HER

PAULA McLAIN

New Issues Press

WESTERN MICHIGAN UNIVERSITY

for Connor

Contents

Less of Her   5

one

Forbidden Planet   9
Take Away   10
Lost in Space   12
Fishing   14
Boardwalk   15
Banquet of the Starved   18
Rider Unhorsed and Bewitched   19

two

Ground Zero   23
Star Thistle   24
Willing   25
Bloom   26
Freight and Groove   27
In My Body, I Am All Eyes   28
Beauty, That Lying Bitch   29
Any Minor World   30

three

Efficiency	35
Parked	36
Less Naked	37
Appetite	38
Made Legible	39
Single in Thebes	41
Collusion	42
Homeopathy	43
Home Remedy	44

four

Yellow	49
Revision with Pastel	50
More	51
Letter to Umbria	52
Consolation	53
My Seven Mice	54
Residue	55
Not Drowning but Waving	56
Connor in the Wind and Rain with His Coat on	57
Mercy	58
Notes	60

Acknowledgments

Versions of these poems first appeared in:

The Alembic: "Less Naked," "Efficiency"

The Bellingham Review: "Any Minor World"

Cream City Review: "Homeopathy"

Green Mountains Review: "Less of Her"

Third Coast: "Lost in Space," "Bloom"

Quarterly West: "Boardwalk"

"Beauty, That Lying Bitch" was the inspiration for a collection of siren and mermaid texts set to music by composer Eric Moe, first performed at The University of Pittsburgh, February 21, 1999.

I would like to thank the MacDowell Colony and Vermont Studio Center for residencies during which many of these poems were written, and the Meijer Foundation and The Putney School for their support.

Thanks, as well, to the many friends who have read these poems, especially Glori Simmons, Michael Schwartz, Scott Beal, Matt Howard, Bruce Smith, Chard deNiord, Harry Bauld and Terence Mickey.

Less of Her

I'd rather tell you about the waist-high grasses,

starred heads of thistle set rocking by our steps,
sleep in the finger-crook of a fig tree and mottled light
like monarchs stirring her hair.

I would say, *Our eyes are fig round.*

I would say, *The violet spine of Indian paintbrush
is more than I remember.*

But a story comes to my window
and it does not speak of willow
or the bodies of low hills.

It has her shadow-damaged face.
It is riddled with bruises the size of his fingertips.

Every time it comes, there is less of her.

Girl: A word I'd offer if she were anything
but a flinch, now, fricative as hard talk.

When I dream about her, the story is redder
and less true: our father's head split smile-wide
by the right rock, his blood threading saplings
to settle in the low spots.

There is nothing to hold her in place,
nothing to whittle her smaller. She climbs the hill,

thrumming wheat stalks with her new hands,
making everything sing.

one

Where is she vanishing? . . . A girl, almost . . . .

—Rilke

Forbidden Planet

Stacks away, a boy is telling another boy about not dancing
but digging past taffeta to panties. She's damp but stops him,
half-giggles a "hmm mm."

Books are leaking history and must. I'm soft with it.

At the dance I stuffed yellow mints into the fingers of my gloves.
Couples spun and shuffled. The globe spit glitter.

I begin with the Q's, attend only to dust motes, paper cuts.

I know, for instance, that ballerinas have horned feet, claws really;
that my mother will find those boy's jeans
under my sister's bed. Beauty has always been suspicious.

Bumble-bee was once *humble-bee*. Unlikely flier.

The housefly's legs, so delicately haired,
can stick to any surface
(rotten plum, slick skin, the moon's pitted profile)
and take away something it can use.

Take Away

Barbados, circa 1812

There rests on my high sill a reed cane of sugar,
cut and blessed by a boy who loves me
and so is afraid. I will not leave these sheets
for even the moon's audible promise. My pores are a sieve
for vapors. With every sleep I become less frail.

Clothtilde comes with a tureen of fat-dotted broth,
black bread, new greens with oil and plum vinegar.
She watches me, then lifts my gown to stroke
my stomach like a jar just filled with preserves.
Her hand is chamois, a coo—but she may as well
be spooning clouds. My skin has thinned into cheesecloth
I can press anything through: tongue, knot,
most private sinew.

                    *

I was born with a push into my father's hands.
Like Midas he is hard; everything beneath him becomes so.
He crawls into my ear to deposit the unwanted kiss
of his thoughts. He has pocketed safe dreaming.
I labor as a daughter owned outright.

I was six, perhaps, when I knew my mother
could teach me nothing of how to sustain a self.
Any look can deliver her fingers to her neck. She's nervousness,
a scurrying—like the fire ants I've watched construct
a miniature of hell: mouths frantic, they moisten, roll, push—
until grains of sand are as unmanageable
as their own jeweled bellies.

*

The thinning has not given me visions
but Clothtilde does not stop asking *Who waits, child?*
She kneads vanilla into my heels and hands. Wanting to please her
I smile like a sickle with no hunger for the long grass between us.
She combs my hair with her fingers, snips the ends
into a charm for this body heavy only with intention.

Tonight I can hear the sea. It is saying, with a tenuous patience,
that hollow can unstop song. If I were cane emptied of meat—
my spine of sugar—I might straddle wind. The tide
is tired of its cradle: it climbs, rattling stars.

Lost in Space

One

My sister becomes a potato bug.
She's balled, a smallness our mother
can't smack at so she's left there: armadillo,
armored shiver, island fourteen avocado squares
from the kitchen sink. Star Trek gets louder
in the living room; a series of shrill whistles signals
alien understanding.

Two

Me: an ugly girl in a bus window, scowling
at an ugly girl on the curb. Every dog-eared page
in my book is a place I won't have to be again.
I scuff my shoe toes, tug at my eyebrows,
wait to be deposited with the other secret monsters.

My sister's young enough for the jungle gym.
She scales its split bubble, rockets toward the haze
stars live behind. The chain link between us spells a fog.

Three

My mother finds me leaning at the front door.
The peep hole dents my forehead with a better eye.
She's a ghoul, too. Three a.m. she's making things safe,
flicking now on—now off—kitchen light, dome-light,
coffee pot: an SOS the neighbors snore through.

"Go to bed," she says, but I can only blink. My sheets
keep coughing me out. Orphaned by gravity, I dog paddle
the asteroid belt, elbowing TV trays and the frozen sofa,
tracing, in space dust, *she never touches me.*
If this were just about hate I could sleep now.

Fishing

Dos Palos, California 1979

Two girls on a ditch bank
hang spark plugs with hogfat
and wait—for crawfish, suckerfish,
something to take hold. Brown water
tugs a fist of tarweed downstream. The soil
pebbles under and between them.
Bait stiffens at their feet.

They have touched each other and later
touch themselves thinking of this.
One will marry because she never
knew her mother and cannot believe
she is beautiful. She clutches bitterness
like a dream of missing teeth, does not forgive
even the sky for its slow faults.

The other will find herself lost
in the underside of the tongue
of the first boy who will kiss her,
the way some can never recover
from kindness. But now, see how
her sweet skin could break even the moon's
concentration. Ruin is the evening star
bobbing like a cast hook, the echo
of their earliest question.

Boardwalk

Santa Cruz, California 1987

Arcade

"You're alone. You're beautiful. I'd like to photograph you just this way."
Half asleep, I blink: the Giant Dipper arcs from his shoulder
like a half-moon in scaffold. The boardwalk's dizzy
with kids renting the day for five dollars. They're eager to trade up:
five rubber spiders for a blue-tongued frog;
three frogs for the walrus big as my torso.

I want nothing more than to be beautiful. So I lie back,
let him freeze me in the seeing. The clicking of the shutter
echoes the arcade's taffy arm, the sound of shells growing
smaller with each wave's paw.

Ledge

Blue light, yellow light, lenses glossed with vaseline.
A pink camisole's wrenched down past my ribs.
I'm headless. I'm breasts with shadows like vacuums.
In a room fifteen floors above the shoreline I wish myself thinner
on the granite ledge. I'm told to point my toe, flex my calf,
imagine a gold ball warming the small of my back.
I shiver, I'm told to think about sex. "Don't look down," he says.

Prints

If he'd hit me, I'd leave. This is what I tell myself
as he adjusts the flash, asks me to try another face.
The bed's water rocks me into something like sleep
so when I feel him pull the sheet from me,
his belly sagging into mine, I don't even open my eyes.

He nudges a photo through developer until the grays rise
and fix into this: his head between my breasts
as if it were pinned there. The darkroom is valentine-tinged.
I leave him there and go to bed, though it's early afternoon
and I can't remember the last time I was tired.
His sheets smell like a three-day rain.
I can't brush the sand from the pillow.

Ledge

I lean against a car in the parking lot of the Dream Inn,
feeling, even here, the small thunder of campers on the wharf
where sea lions bark and dive for candy apples
and hot dog buns. All the way down the beach, lifeguard stations
are like origami cranes. Who would see the flag of my hand
if I stopped resisting the asphalt's undertow?

The boardwalk is a blur of children.
Lines of them ribbon away from every good ride.
I only go down at night, and take the skyway back and forth
from the arcade to the running green lights of the water slide.

I swing my feet and close my eyes until I can single out each noise
from the roar below. What I'm hearing now is the carnival arc
of a dime into a glass dish. It lands thin and silver: small winnings.

Banquet of the Starved

The maitre d' sniffs as if he's guessed
the way you began for this world: pod girl, monster,
passed like mashed potatoes from a hand in Fort Worth
to a grimace in Queens. Every table invites at least one
who could be your mother, the fetal you
cashew-sized and teased to vanish
under an ashy pouf of hair.

How readily this becomes your hell,
the paisley-clotted walls, the waiting to be served.
You're stuck now. The room's a menu
and you have to choose: *who to sing the lullaby,*
who to rock you irreparably under?

One holds a salad fork as if she's trying to support
its flagging pulse. Another coughs and recrosses her legs.
What were you doing those borrowed nights?
Face it, you'd make a pet of any dead thing, keening
for the punch-out sun. The bats dive-bombing
your childhood weren't knitting, with each echoed pass, a net.
They were feeding.

A woman begins to sob. She sags toward her goblet
like the heartstarved, the hardly forgiven.
She's humming now, a fragment you recognize
as the summer of your thirteenth year.

But your own table waits, the service dealt
like a billiards game begun at your birth. The cloth, yanked
by even your lost, your sleeping, fingers, would unsettle nothing.
You are ruinous, secure. Go on. Reach for the platter:
hazardous mouth: collapsible shore.

Rider Unhorsed and Bewitched

I take the dry ditch at a canter—
fifteen—green felt hat with limpid star uncharted.
I will not wear my glasses for this: lover in the ravel
of cattails, couplet of hoofbeat like stitches
mending drought.

Grasshoppers morse from blonde ground level,
the ash tree arches, unstrung. Fifteen,
I thought I had learned my body. My first trot knocked
at the hard plum of my center, forcing pulse
and precision, drum-rise and repeat: my hips
unhinged to mouth *hello.*

Fifteen (as if I'd weathered it), my father
shows me how to kiss. *Not that way,* he wipes my lips.
Sleep snaps: my piebald bed, star-puddled,
calamitous. I straddle fifteen, stand blankly,
trace the house with nighttime feet. The window is dry-eyed
as a housewife, tinder for the wholly unforgivable.

two

I was erectile tissue; though mostly, after the manner approved by Plato, I had intercourse by eye.

—William Gass

Ground Zero

The anthill is any red planet, cones and depressions,
grainy soil that with spit might adobe into loaves.
I straighten to recess. An India ball pings
two-square. Kissing happens behind the backstop.
If I stop dragging my pencil through math,
will I get this coupling? The sweaty hands
and aspirant morphography? A whistle bleats.
Mitts thump the end of orbit. Self-spun, I'm cupped
to collapse on my own pulse. Radio-obvious:
pocked: plangent. I sigh and dandelions go solar.

Star Thistle

Isomorph of the acrimonious sun.
Hook-eared and bony as the daughter
whistling for a stray. In her Gesthemane,
distance and thirst lie down next to God
and wait to be kissed. The fig tree leaches green
into papery hands. Evening presses
like a man's belly.

Thistle is soft's opposite, the halo
calcified, cutting teeth. Still, the mare
will snuffle her tender nose, hungry
for precisely this. Imagine her yellow tongue
pierced through, the spines persistent, steepling.

Imagine the daughter stooping to pocket
the image like a stone that might speak back,
then rising again, making her way
toward the house, toes witching dust.

Willing

He says you're a blackberry, dropped into his mouth
by a crow, says *Sweet, sweet girl* to the damp of your neck.
It's afternoon. Through your squint, foxtail splinters,
blonde as the half-slip we fight over in the catalogue,
the demi-cup bra, satin-strapped and less candid
than this boy's hands. He'd wear you like skin if you'd let him.

He says locusts told him where to find you,
that your blue dress is plenty deep for two;
and you're starting to trust the muscle
all this wanting gives you. Your shoulders come back
when a car full of boys rockets by on the two-lane, pulling dust
and a long howl. All the way out to the interstate,
they talk about turning around.

Now your arm is beside you, bent, like a page you'll return to.
He says *Listen*, then stops talking. What comes next isn't news:
his sudden flush and bloom. Then the cell-like splitting
of this day into two, four, eight identical others.

I pass the shape you've tamped into the grass.
It looks like an animal has circled before sleeping. I lie down,
willing anything: a ripple, rain. I lick my hand.
There is no tinge of blackberry, no hint of what's coming.

Bloom

In the house, chicken skin crackles under knives and forks,
butter softens on white bread. The news hums civilly.

I'm an ear pressed to hard-packed clay where the woodpile breaks
down. Under one split heart, spider eggs are cottony

stops in the sentence I'm reluctant to finish, even now,
when I'm forced to guess if it was fever

or yellow-jacket that buzzed so fitfully between my eyebrows,
fixing a glaze on the table where my sisters

folded their hands and went genuinely ceramic.
It helps to say the creature had wings, was mistaking

my cornea for calyx, rubbing its gloss of pollen on lashes
shut too late, it seems, because the fringe had been sequined,

beaded. And if my eye was not rechristened green
in that thin garden, it parted, steadily, for all that was outside:

for wheat-haired boys under sky, for mesa and the consolation
of insects, for the sun's jeweled fist. Parted:

weedy trapdoor, troubled but industrious center
forcing a second, difficult birth and family in things.

Freight and Groove

> *That Love is all there is,*
> *Is all we know of Love:*
> *It is enough, the freight should be*
> *Proportioned to the groove.*
> —Emily Dickinson

There is no antidote. You look again
on the small bed, its chewed blue spread,
pillow flat as the sigh already behind you.

Scraps of bitten fingernail have needled
through the carpet's nap. Sloughed skin
recomposes in a cone of light.

This country's currency is lint and tugged string.

If you buried your toe and spun to plow back
bruised sleep and dinner voices,
the unstudied smudges on your pane,

no strange thing would pucker from the groove.

Lie down in the drive and hear the phone lines
buzz beyond you. Unsettle a few beetles;
kick a stippled fender.

It will all be too soft and wrong.

Nothing here loves you, your shinbark
and venom, thin howl and toehold.
All your ornamental dark.

In My Body, I Am All Eyes

for Robin

The man at the window will never turn
to face me. His jeans are stiff with sand
and could stand alone.

It is possible that only the pane preserves
him: the sea has serious hands
and—like a lover

for whom grief is a chronic bloom—
can't stop apologizing. Bluing spool
of sofa, the banister's anxious neck:

I can rebuild this room
anywhere, carve its miniature in soap
or pitch, insisting on the same complications—

He never loved me. My witness is a lean
into unflinching detail. Three limes
kiss the formica. Sink water

chalks an outline of fingers splayed—
unforgivably open—and I'm reminded
of a painting: the wife cradles her face

in one palm like a crumpled draft
or half-eaten apple. Her second hand, all eyes,
fishes the empty table.

Beauty, That Lying Bitch

Of course what called you was lovely. A girl gone
milky with rain. You could show me now, couldn't you?
just where her glory of hair teased your belly into brushfire.
Or was it evening and her ass the lit crystal of the living moon?
Don't worry, you weren't the first or most foolish. She smiled
(porcelain curl of calla lily) as she told you the rocks
that would slit you like a herring were worth the song,
the fuck so slow and wrung with stars it would scatter you.
Do your research. The siren is bird and beautiful, but also a sea-cow,
a salamander with lungs on its back—wings shriveled as spent sex.
And here you were thinking ugly only got as loud as you let it.

Any Minor World

The mud-dauber's nest is ugly and efficient,
brown as a summered fist

against the eaves. I save it all.
The wings arrowing out of the tight hole;

my tripping run and sob and kneel;
Mother swabbing camphor on the stings risen

into anthills. By and by, the story gets smaller.
The details, anorexic but increasingly fine:

furred pod of milkweed, buzzing sun,
oranges gone too sweet under skin.

I might unbarricade the narrative altogether,
draw several lines in the air between my mother and me,

label one of the lines "you," who stand, for now,
outside all of this, either watching or not.

We could walk the long drive, count together
each blossom on the wild mustard,

but these trees will never be cottonwood.
History constricts, leaves story like a throat caught

in dry swallow. This holds:
my mother swings the broom back. Her hands

grip the straw, and I hear such small snapping.
I don't flinch. Like the fiddle-spider

rounding the window's edge with web,
I'm almost still and still there.

three

At length my cry was known:
Therein lay my release.
I met the wolf alone
And was devoured in peace.

—Edna St. Vincent Millay

Efficiency

I was just dreaming the note
before a kiss. My mouth was twice its size,
lipsticked, unmistakable. Then morning
ruined everything, birdsong fractured as a plate
no charming hostess would leave in the hutch.

If I could wade out of my pillow
I wouldn't need these magazines.

If I had a man I could stop answering
every quiz with *all of the above*. I could forsake
morning altogether and the violin swell
that has become my afternoon.
Bliss would be pity uncomposed.
These simple knots left to the weather.

I wouldn't need a man if I could summon
sufficient tragedy, devise a plot to leave myself
at the altar. The pipe organ would do all the sobbing;
the congregation could save their hankies
for airplanes and origami swans.

I'd be in the anteroom, all froth
and panic, my hair a stiff meringue.
I'd harass the daisies until one finally swore love,
while miles away, on unfragile asphalt,
my true future, my groom, would be dismantling
speed and shine, letting ashes blow back
onto the upholstery, forgetting.

Parked

An avalanche of orange blossoms, the crippled moon.
Over his shoulder, furrows rippled and pitched.
Fruit nubby from fingering. Sour.

Yellow light wept like someone's Jesus or rain
in the French Quarter. When I say "our"
I mean very little. Damp hands and static.

Vinyl sticky as a table set years before.
I'd like to milk a bell for every ant at my picnic,
the whimsical champing of their mandibles,

legs like cartoon sickles under the vanishing cake.
Where's sixteen? I ate it—and sentiment. Cotton girl
in all-cotton panties like a flag for what sadness?

The tease is that I can spit it out like this,
easy as seeds in the crosshatch of tire tracks
as the car rocks through soft decay, taking me home.

Less Naked

He follows, seeing the way trees fall away from her,
thinking *recession of birches,* thinking
a bit of bark carefully peeled might make fine paper.
It's not that she loves him or will not survive
the way he labels the arc of her hand rising
to brush a moth from his face even before the moth startles.
They walk a path someone else has cleared. Pine needles
knit to form what is not a carpet. She hums privately.
When they reach a hollow place, she removes her blouse
and lies down, knowing leaves will catch in her hair
like something unfinished and that he will not remove them.

Appetite

The mice have been at our books again. They know
everything about us, how in our low beds,
still blind and stained with sleep, we begin mewling.
Wednesday delivers tender feet and elbows.
We bump into ourselves coming back from the bathroom.

Through vaginal cracks along the baseboard,
the delicate tines of their own whiskers, the young ones
study our breakfasting: the table nearly balanced
as we dilute and stir, buttering sad toast.
Our crumbs represent us entirely.

In our absence the mice do no cartoon rejoicing,
they fuck, scratching ideograms for appetite
into our headboard. One spends her litter
on the ravaged dictionary. By the time her babies
plump to the size of our thumbs, each will have eaten
more than we can say.

Made Legible

1.

His kiss is kamikaze, pinning her
to the kid leather until her hips begin to bleat.
Say my name. She'll smell their sex for two days;
wear the bitten nipple, blue fist of a bruise. *Say it.*

2.

When Swinburne misnamed a rhythm, his schoolmaster
struck the true stress into his palms,
waking meter in the welt.

The body can be made legible.
Our scholar grew insomniac, studying himself,
the subcutaneous text nearly brilliant.

He pined for the right reader: a boy part scribe, part scarab,
love-starved to acuity. His thrusts would be scansion, each sob
unstopping body that was bottle for the message
halved and halved again and still too large.

3.

If my nails score you cleanly.

If what I leave on your hands stiffens to resemble
a phrase you scribbled to yourself in salt at twenty.

If I fuck you like I'd fuck myself.

4.

As a girl I was quietly losing gravity: *If no one holds me,*
how am I held to earth?

It took a mirror to find the shape of my mother's hand
above my knee's crease, the rays of yellow-white like a spine
for the swelling.

5.

He stops and stops at one o' clock on her clitoris,
needing her to forget she has ribs,
to say just once what she wants. She falls into his mouth,
bilingual, breath-stopped.

6.

Shut up unless you would damn yourself to be loved.

Single in Thebes

It's not enough that I live in a city where doom rents billboard space and violence is the tired pestilence of bodies denting themselves to prove they aren't stone. Now the news insists I'm not alone. Sixty-four percent of us are freezing tears for the New Year's Eve we'll spend under our kitchen tables. Loneliness has gone condo. I limp home: neon repeats unremarkable rain, faces clenched with giveaway. I believed grief, its dig and drone reliable as the cavities that will form in a mouth sucking on the tongue's simple sugar. I masturbate until my fingers stiffen and still smell only exhaust, the rinse of legitimate agonies. Stacked, they'd babble through every empty cab and stoop, the cat's cradle of wires on the bridge we're lined up to fling ourselves from. Just now a woman screamed. I don't think it was me.

Collusion

This landscape is loaded.
Sob of a sunset, the path cut to uncover
hoofprints like pulled moons.

See how the maple's knot never softens—
girl with a lavender slash at her throat.

We slow for September—yellow dust and sputter—
her knack for subtraction. Unmoored, we forget
that in May the ferns were like buttons.

I'll never, you say, or think it
and your hand falls between us like a nest

between two poplars. Shall I wrestle leaves?
Read string and straw as blueprints
for knitting? Would I step from the blue grass

of my own too-kissed skin?
We are standing too long in the meadow.
And we are not fireflies, not ciphers, not snow.

Homeopathy

The man howling at the rain on Amsterdam might diagnose
love, but we press heads and agree: it's viral. The fever
should be starved, your flushed hands stuffed into socks.
If we empty the bed of all but you, the sheet is a blind grid.
Shuttle your feet toward cool. For nausea, try to isolate
each of the forty-three muscles it takes to build the face
your father would call resolute, your mother sincere.
For sleep, imagine that as I leave your city I am any woman,
inconstant as the light that has traveled seven minutes
to your window from a star that could not be surprised
by distrust. If it gives you small peace, imagine me paused
at a stoplight. Not lost, not reeling. The mattress is navigable;
exhale to impress a new seriousness. If you wake unwell,
gargle salt and ash while remembering you have not waited for this.

Home Remedy

I smoothed and blocked my hands like a shirt in a gift box.
Snow fell, soiled. Ice released the house.
My son began to walk—I know this now—
but everything came to me through water. His cry
was a bubble breaking just past me.

I slumped to the floor in the pantry,
head resting on a bag of heat-softened vidalias,
but then there were the baseboards to consider,
and the industry of black ants in my white rice.
I got up.

It took me half a day to walk to the refrigerator,
but once I was there I knew why.
I faced the labels of the mustard, the marmalade,
the baby gherkins. I filled the ice trays,
set a flank steak out to thaw.

In this way the days pass: the TV speaks to the spin cycle.
I can make the dishes last three hours, passing my index nail
inside the tines and over the knotted flowers
on the flat of each fork. *Trillium*, I want to say,
but they could be footprints,

some tiny thing letting me know it's been here all along.

four

I started out as a girl
without a shadow, in iron shoes;
now, at the end of the world
I am a woman full of rain.
The journey back should be easy;
if this reaches you, wait for me.

—Lisel Mueller

Yellow

Nothing but sun outside, stubborn shrapnel
hissing *choose.* She leans: her face a plate, tongue on a stem.

How many months has the moon been an abacus?

When she walks, it is a kind of unswaddling, into air
stung with her sister's goodness,
into the orchard, the road, expectancy.

The day has forsythia underpinnings: yellow
caught with the offings of things that begin and begin.

Her father swims in her pocket like a cufflink, like change
that won't be spent. With a little pressure, we can see this moment
as perforated, a seam without remorse.

Fresno will detach, dissolve—and her seventeenth year,
and the word *daughter.*

We would tell her to keep something for herself,

creased in a sweaty shoe; that she might know these potholes
as tide pools, the nearly forgotten life
rubbed smaller, buried, then pitched into sun again.

Revision with Pastel

She meets a painter who exposes only faces
in pastel on plywood, masonite, paper towel.
A boy with river-hair shadows her from the studio,
shrinks to rest on the hard bed of her molar,
persisting there like chocolate gone bitter.

For days she doesn't sleep, then it hits her: she's in love.
Fever and paleness. How strange her face is,
and luminous. She fixates on her slender arm,
the reach of it quite lavender now.
Her nail beds are pinched with saffron.

The lover may be missing but she continues
to melt, dapple. Her neck is willow, her thigh
a shell-pink trellis. She is now in full recline,
exactly herself but roomier, less stained by impression.
Her lashes wax heliotropic. She beads, she lingers.

More

It is not enough that yearly, down this hill,
April comes like an idiot, babbling and strewing flowers.
— Edna St. Vincent Millay

Our April was preamble, guilt-kissed,
precipitous—daffodils set on stun.

We romanced the solstice. A new moon spooned
tenor sax. Of course there was dancing,

but more inhabitable is the pillowsack of lint
that, gathered daily, catalogues our wobbling arc.

This is how it's done: the call comes too late
to be anything but a choked *more*.

I've ingested your sloughed cells: the miniature you
night-blooms in a bronchial forest.

Letter To Umbria

for Michael

I came too early: there are no fireflies in my meadow.
Insect bites rise into speech on my neck and shoulders.

In two days they will be gone. Are you napping in a cathedral?
Making sense of some lovely fountain, thinking

this stone is as large as my hand, this fish floats like a lung?
Last night a bat showed me the space between two trees.

There was no comet in the frame or its echo.
I thought I would fall down from sighing.

Let's not say that this is unlikely: the moon has been full
since you left. The flower moon, I was told, and believed

I saw particles stray from the blown face.
Are there ferns in your country and blackbirds?

Do moths move in your periphery so that you think of my skin
in the bath? Late spring has seduced New Hampshire:

I can stop hoarding dust and eyelashes. Blessedly,
there is no remedy for this pining. I sleep with two-thirds of you.

Consolation

Two women in pink light.
Face powder puddles on a silk shoulder.
The letter, creased and recreased, perches
on the settee like a wounded bird.
This is loss but opulent: damp violets and a glove,
polite cough from an interior room.

The lover is utterly gone. She'll receive his uniform
starched, in a box worthy of it. It will feel like new grass
and smell nothing like his neck or wrists
buried all those afternoons in her hair.

Yet even the crush of her crinoline,
the way she swoons into consolation is beautifully
fogged, defying particularity—
like one of Strand's early photos: marsh, tree bark
and horizon soft-sponged into a single texture—
as if tears themselves will keep a lens untrue.

How much do we need to see? How stark the line?
How spent the face?

I come upon my mother sleeping:
her cotton housedress up around her thighs, pale hair
crowding a dime-sized mole, chickenpox scars.
Already her stingy heart gurgles. The tumors
in her throat grow gauzy.

I'll be nine years revising
her terrible hands, nine more finding mercy
enough to nurse my own pockmarks and depressions.
She snores thickly. I have so few dead, I nearly love her.

My Seven Mice

My mice nest in my wedding dress.
They nose through the blind sleeves
leaving pellets like seed pearls
on the unfine satin. (It's not something
I'd wear again.) They're the second shift,
navigators of pipe and perfect shadow,
minding my business and their own
which is residue, excess, dawn's collar
and curfew. I don't knit them sweaters
but I've driven them to Phoenix—
two thousand miles of sand flats,
cornfield militia, the bald dark—and I could see
the new life spin out like a cotillion.
I entered the desert thinking *okay.*
Hope is an agreeable thirst.
Then a forest of saguaro moved into my headlights.
Tell me the shy, the minor misery
of those arms isn't enough to send anyone
back to the city, to waking like a cramp
in the single bed, three a.m. scuttle and claw:
assurance that yes, we're each alone
with our seven mice, our thimblefuls of sugar,
our poison of nearly enough.

Residue

Not such a sad story: the woman wakes to an observation.
She's become a clear needle; thin enough, finally, to pick her own lock.
She takes with her one pair of tight shoes, a light bulb,
a line on her brow for every time she's given birth.
There will be moments of guilt in gas station bathrooms,
but no postcards from Omaha or Orange County: *Wish you were.*
Her daughters still have the polestar, their own freckled noses.
If pressed she would describe the long door closing with a cough
of dust and feathers. Not the seventeen blocks to the station,
strap of her bag spelling a new fate; not the way the fire escapes
sagged with their own weight as if to say *just jump.*
If she's learned anything it's that specifics stir everyone up. Exhaust
leaves enough residue for a sketch of her general shape
in a back window. The bus shifts into full groan, vanishing messily.

Not Drowning But Waving

As a girl, I held midnight by one stumpy leg
and dragged it room to room. A moon
thick as Hitchcock as I called *goodnight*
to see if even the hated would answer *here.*

Night sky was easily the Pacific exacting her price,
my sisters moored to coral, wet and decorous.
Water hammered my ears with years of answers.

How many practice dives?
(Once my mother's swollen face
and a depression in sand begging milk.)
How many stones sewn into the skirt?

Once the absolute *under* of dread akin to love—
thick and finned and toothy—or sirocco
coughing blue sand over the wearisome stars.

Now my hand: buoyant, pale as seaweed
in a night that could have been painted by a child.
(Acrylic lover dozing on his well-lit train.)
Now: the sheets glow audibly, the appliances.

Every sorry heart in the city
is suddenly a neighbor and awake.

Connor in the Wind and Rain with His Coat on

Connor is four and every day brings a clutch
of clouds that shift when we say *elephant, wolf dancing
in a stand of trees, rabbit unpinning his tail again.*
Mornings begin several times before breakfast.
Numbers are still malleable enough to describe
the perfect stick, the way rocks find one another for balance.
His mother wants to blow him words like *Pakistan* and *chamomile*
and *gosling.* His father can become anyone at all. They are able
to forget everything but the way Connor clung to her belly
minutes after he was born, rooting like a sweet newt,
craning to display the small "c" of his marvelous ear,
and they knew they could stop waiting for their lives.

Mercy

Forget: what he said, the gas station
where you wadded and sobbed,
the dank mirror and drain.

It's frightening and simple: more
would have left you with a manageable face.
You didn't have more.

Dear girl, you began as a liquid. Your mother
could not unthink you.

Splashing between your own knees
in the bath was tidally governed. You gurgled
and burped. Who could admonish
the seahorse of your green toe?

Soap-stung, emptied by accident
you've ridden the unlivable like a bike
with missing kickstand.

Forget: smoke, revision. Your story
cannot blind you, nor can it usher you out.

Let the others bet their matchsticks on the present.
Unwarm, less permeable than prayer,
this porcelain can be coral, carapace, slow shell.

Rest here among the fist-sized bits
of you. Lean into the ruminant furniture, your dead,

the landscape which has never been behind
but will bear your weight, your wet,
your loud look home.

Notes

The speaker in "Take Away" is based on Dary Chase, the daughter of a wealthy nineteenth century plantation owner in Barbados. Over a period of six years, she starved herself to death to escape her father's cruelty.

"Rider Unhorsed and Bewitched" is a title taken from a Klee pen and ink; "Banquet of the Starved" from James Ensor's painting.

The title "In My Body, I Am All Eyes" is borrowed from Edmund Jabes' *The Book of Yukel:* "The eye lets us see what it hears, tastes, touches. In my body, I am all eyes."

"My Seven Mice" grew out of a conversation I had with another resident at the MacDowell Colony. He was having trouble sleeping because the mice in his studio were making so much noise at night. Over a period of several days, he caught seven of them in a store-bought trap and was certain his trouble was over—for life, in fact, since he insisted there were seven mice for every human on the planet.

The introductory image in "Consolation" was suggested by Alfred Stevens' painting, "After the Ball".

Epigraphs found on these pages are from the following publications:

p. 7
Rilke, Rainer Maria. *The Selected Poems*: Trans. Stephen Mitchell. New York, Vintage International, 1989.

p. 21
Gass, William. *In the Heart of the Heart of the Country, and other stories*. New York: Harper & Row, 1968.

p. 27
Dickinson, Emily. *Selected Poems.* Ed. Christopher Moore.
New York: Park Lane Press, 1993.

pp. 33, 51
Millay, Edna St. Vincent. *Selected Poems.* Ed. Colin Falck.
New York, Harper Perennial, 1992.

p. 47
Mueller, Lisel. *Alive Together: New and Selected Poems.*
Baton Rouge: Louisiana State University Press, 1996.

photo by Danner Bradshaw

Paula McLain is a native of Fresno, California. In 1997, she received her MFA in poetry from the University of Michigan, where she was the recipient of a Meijer Foundation Award. She has been a work-study scholar at Bread Loaf, and a resident at The MacDowell Colony and Vermont Studio Center. Currently she is working on a collection of essays about the fourteen years she and her two sisters spent as foster children in California. For the last few years she has taught in Vermont, but has recently returned to Ann Arbor.

New Issues Press Poetry Series

James Armstrong, *Monument in a Summer Hat*

Anthony Butts, *Fifth Season*

Gladys Cardiff, *A Bare Unpainted Table*

Lisa Fishman, *The Deep Heart's Core Is a Suitcase*

Lance Larsen, *Erasable Walls*

David Dodd Lee, *Downsides of Fish Culture*

Deanne Lundin, *The Ginseng Hunter's Notebook*

David Marlatt, *A Hog Slaughtering Woman*

Paula McLain, *Less of Her*

Malena Mörling, *Ocean Avenue*

Julie Moulds, *The Woman With a Cubed Head*

Marsha de la O, *Black Hope*

Rebecca Reynolds, *Daughter of the Hangnail*

John Rybicki, *Traveling at High Speeds*

Diane Seuss-Brakeman, *It Blows You Hollow*

Marc Sheehan, *Greatest Hits*

Angela Sorby, *Distance Learning*

Russell Thorburn, *Approximate Desire*

Patricia Jabbeh Wesley, *Before the Palm Could Bloom:*
 Poems of Africa